Deeply Hurt, Deeply Wounded and Deeply Violated!

By Rachell Clark

Order this book online at www.trafford.com
or email orders@trafford.com

Most Trafford titles are also available at major online book retailers.

Print information available on the last page.

ISBN: 978-1-4269-1370-9 (sc)

Trafford rev. 08/18/2020

www.trafford.com
North America & international
toll-free: 1 888 232 4444 (USA & Canada)
fax: 812 355 4082

This is the true story of Rachell Clark struggles and childhood life of pain and how she triumphed over her enemies. All of the names have been changed except for Ms. Thomas and my Grandparents.

This book is about many unfortunate events that happened in my life as a child and young adult. I want to talk a little bit about my grandmother and grandfather. My grandmother's maiden name was Lizzie Goings she was born in Charms, Virginia, on January 31st 1907. My grandmother had her first child when she was just a young girl—not by choice but as the result of rape by a Caucasian man. In those days, black girls were not protected under the law from sexual predators.

My uncle looked very different from my grandmother's other children. He could pass for Caucasian. My grandfather's name was Bufford Luster; born on October 19th, 1889, in Nashville, Tennessee. My grandfather met my grandmother; they fell in love, got married and had eight children together. My grandfather became an alcoholic and died around 1955. Heavy drinking in any family will destroy it. I saw a picture of my grandfather and grandmother. My grandfather was holding a whip in his hand which he beat his own children. It looked very scary in his hand.

As far as I know, all my uncles were alcoholics and almost all of my aunts were alcoholics, too. My mother was not a heavy drinker, but she was a pothead, and later in her life, she became addicted to crack cocaine. One of my mom's sisters who I did not see very often had a son named Jonathan. He was a [1]severe alcoholic. My family was poor, and reared their children on welfare. I was rejected long before I was born.

When my mother was sixteen, she met a much older man and ran off with him to New York. He turned her out on the streets. My mother started doing drugs and became a prostitute. One day in New York, this (mystery) man got angry with her and beat her in the head with a baseball bat. It did not kill her, but she suffered brain damage as a result. My mother was never the same after that man beat her. I believe this tragedy happened in her life because he thought she owed him money. The love of money is the root of all evil."

My mother made her way back to Cleveland in a horrible state of mind. It is hard for me to imagine what that must have been like for her. From that, point on my mother was in and out of mental institutions due to her mental state. My mother started living from state to state. Nobody ever knew where she was. My mother was determined not to go back in a mental institution. There were terrible things done to her there that she could not talk about freely. She moved back to Cleveland in her late twenties.

My mother met this married man named Blake. They were going strong for a while until she got pregnant with me in 1968. He left her as some men do after they have had their fill of sexual pleasure. My mother told her family that she was pregnant, but nobody believed her until she showed them proof. She was still very much unstable—financially and mentally. When my mother was ready to give birth to me in the hospital, the doctor told her family that she could

---

[1]   God has given me victory over poverty.

never take care of me because of her state of mind. When I was born, the doctor ran a series of tests on me to determine if I was a normal baby. I stayed in the hospital for ten days before they released me. I was already [2] labeled just another statistic of society. How many of you know that it is not where you come from, it is where you're going? You do not have to be a victim of your circumstances. You can be an over comer. You can over come your circumstances!

My Aunt Lisa took me from the hospital when the doctor released me. Lisa's husband did not want me as his daughter. They already had four boys of their own and another child on the way. I believe strongly that I was rejected because of the circumstances I was born into. My arrival brought division and confusion in their marriage. I believe at that time my aunt had the best intentions for me.

Six months after I was born my aunt had a beautiful baby girl. As toddlers, we sometimes dressed alike. My cousin and I were very close—like sisters. Lisa and her husband started having some serious marital problems and I believed I was partly to blame. I knew I was despised and unwanted.

I always felt like an orphan when I was a child. I always loved my uncle like a father, and I was always seeking his approval in my life as the father I so desperately needed. I never got his approval or the love I was seeking.

One day my uncle told my aunt that, he was leaving Cleveland to go to California to find a better job and that he would send for his family when he was settled. Weeks went by. Then months went by and my aunt did not hear from her husband. In the mean time, my aunt got involved with another man named Jay. I saw this man get very violent with her when she broke it off with him. Lisa still loved her husband very much! We were living in a fairly poor neighborhood. I was around five years old when a man saw me playing outside and took me to this abandoned building where he raped and tormented me. He told me that if I told anyone he would kill me or hurt me so badly no one would recognize me. This man raped me on [3]more than one occasion. I was so afraid to tell anybody that I was being sexually violated. I decided to keep this horrible secret in the dark because of my shame, guilt and low self-esteem. I was so paralyzed with fear that I blocked this out for many years. This is what can happen to your children when they are not being supervised. I believe this man was a friend of the family. When this horrible ordeal came back to my remembrance, I felt the pain all over again—just like it was yesterday. I asked the Lord to forgive him and save his soul from hell fire.

My Aunt Lisa packed us up in a station wagon to move to California to find her husband. When we arrived, she did not know where her husband was. She finally found him through his social security number. He was working at the Holiday Inn.

We lived in the station wagon for weeks because she did not have money for a hotel. After my uncle found out we were there, he did the right thing and put us up in a hotel—only out of obligation, nothing else. My uncle did not want to play the husband or father role anymore. I believe my uncle wanted to be totally free from his responsibility to his wife and children. My uncle already had another woman when we got to California. The woman he had gotten involved with did not have any children and he fell in love with her. My uncle divorced my aunt and married this other woman. My uncle shut his own children out of his life after he married. His four boys felt

---

[2]   I am a walking miracle!

[3]   God hath not given us a spirit of fear, but of power, and of love and of a sound   mind. 2 Tim 1:7

completely abandoned by their father, but he still maintained some relationship with his daughter. He came to pick her up occasionally and even brought her money and gifts sometimes.

I was always treated differently from my cousin. Her needs were always met. I never got the things she got—new clothes, a bike, money, love, protection. I was glad [4] that she was able to get all these things, but I did not have the same privileges she did. I always felt like an outcast in the family.

One time my uncle came over to take us to Universal Studios. Unfortunately, I never got to go because I supposedly did something wrong and was being punished. I had to stay in the house all day while my cousin was having the best time of her life. I felt so abandoned, empty and deeply hurt.

When I was about seven years old, my cousins began molesting and raping me. My cousins were older and stronger than I was. They also started torturing me by putting a butter knife over a hot flame and placing it on my arm, leaving a bad burn on my upper right arm that is there to this day. I still did not understand why I was being abused and violated by members of my own family. My Aunt Lisa was hardly ever around to supervise what was going on in the home. Everybody was out for themselves, including the two girls, I and my cousin. My aunt partied all the time. She started drinking and did not care about life too much after her husband divorced her. It was as if she had given up on life!

This has happened to more than just one woman in my family. There have been at least three women in my family that became mentally ill over a man. Never make a man your whole life. He can never take the place of the true and living God! We are supposed to love our husbands, pray for them, and tend to their needs. However, they should never be allowed to dominate us or take the place of God.

Aunt Lisa got to the point of dropping us off at the park every single day and did not return to pick us up until nighttime. The park was our regular baby sitter. The only things we had to eat consistently were cookies and sandwiches, and we drank juice. Sometimes I went hungry with no food to eat.

[5] One day I was at home, hungry with nothing to eat except miracle whip and a few pieces of bread. I made a miracle whip sandwich and was still hungry. When I was nine years old, I was at home alone with nothing to eat. There was food in the house but it had to be cooked. I went into the freezer and pulled out some chicken, defrosted it, seasoned it and baked it. I opened a can of cream of chicken soup, poured it on the chicken, and stuck it back in the oven. I cooked some rice and corn to go with it. The meal turned out to be very good and everybody enjoyed it. Unfortunately, I had to grow up very fast in order to survive.

By the time I reached ten years old my aunt had grown very tired of me. I became a burden to her. Aunt Lisa walked in on her son having unconsentual sex with me and said nothing. She was supposed to protect me—instead she hurt me even more. The next thing I knew, my aunt packed a bag for me and put me on a Greyhound bus with only ten dollars to my name. That was a three-day bus ride from L.A. to Cleveland. I was so terrified being on that bus alone at the age of ten. I did not know how to change from one bus to the next. This one woman on her way to Buffalo, New

---

[4] But seek ye first the kingdom of God, and His righteousness; and all these things shall be added unto you. Matthew 6:33

[5] …Man shall not live by bread alone, but by every word that proceedeth out of the mouth of God. Matt: 4:4

York realized I was riding the bus alone and helped me. This Good Samaritan woman let me ride on the bus next to her, and she bought me food with her own money. She protected me like one of Gods angels. I will never forget the love and concern this woman showed for me.

I made it safely to Cleveland and my Uncle Wilson picked me up from the Greyhound bus station. I thought things would get better for me after I got to Cleveland. I was wrong. I started living with my Aunt Annette, her husband, her two grown daughters and her son. They partied all the time and had men over to the house that got drunk. My cousin's boyfriends were always trying to have sex with me. This goes back to what happened to [6] me in California. My Aunt Lisa called Cleveland telling my family how bad I was and that I was sexually active. She told them that I had seduced her son. My aunt's son raped me and he was around nineteen years old. My aunt ruined my reputation with my family by protecting her son. Among my family members and their friends, my name was ruined. I was just a young girl that nobody cared about. No one taught me what was right. I was all alone to fight the world by myself because no one cared enough to protect me.

One night while everybody was passed out drunk, my cousin's boyfriend forced himself on me and raped me while everybody was sleeping. Then he started doing it on a regular basis. I was scared and too intimidated to tell anybody what was going on. Besides nobody would have believed me! They would have blamed me for what he did wrong. This man had children of his own, was married to another woman; and yet he violated my body. My cousin found out about what he did to me, and she blamed me for what that child molester did to me. My cousin told me I was never going to amount to anything except being a whore. The sad thing about it is that I actually started believing her. Almost every man that came across my path as a child violated me in some form or another. Several members of my own family sexually and mentally abused me.

One day when I was around twelve years old, my cousin, Devon and I were at home alone. He was trying to rape me. I told him no, but that did not stop him from trying. I tried to leave, but Devon was blocking the door to prevent me from leaving! After he held me hostage, he left the door for a brief moment. I opened the door and started running down the stairs. Devon threw a pitchfork at me while I was running down the stairs. This is the same pitchfork he was using to hold me hostage. I was very blessed the fork did not stab me.

[7] Devon always had a troubled life with the law. He started cutting school in kindergarten to stand on the corner and beg for money. After that he began stealing, breaking into cars and he even started a fire. I went and told his mother what he did. Devon came after me to terrorize me and to scare me so I would not tell on him again. He became a regular street hustler including giving oral sex to men for money. Devon has been in and out of jail his whole life. His mother gave him everything he wanted and he turned around and repaid her with evil. Devon's father was an alcoholic and his mother suffered a nervous break down.

My Aunt Annette actually accused me of sleeping with her husband—totally false! I was always accused as a child of doing something wrong. I started living with my grandmother after that happened. My grandmother was living in a two level home that belonged to my uncle and his wife. My grandmother lived upstairs and they lived down stairs. I have a cousin named Mark who was already living with my grandmother, and one day he introduced me to Jesus by asking me if I wanted to receive Him as my personal Savior. I said yes and was saved. For the first time in my life I felt different and I felt the love of God. It saved my life.

---

[6]   I am created in God's image Genesis 1:27 paraphrased

[7]   God will give us a peaceful life if we trust in Him.

My uncle's wife and her mother hated me without a reason. I remember when my uncle beat me because I stayed at my boyfriend's house all night. I would not cry no matter how hard he hit me, so he started hitting me harder. Finally, after I did not cry it scared him and he said, "Get on out of here!" At that point in my life I was determined I was not going to let anybody hurt me ever again. I shut down completely, and built a wall of protection around myself. My uncle came to my grandmother and told her that I could not live there any longer due to his wife. I was homeless after I was put out of my [8] grandmother's house. I went back to my aunt's house to live for a little while even though I did not want to. I had no other place to go. They were still drinking and having parties.

One night when my cousin, Mia was drunk and everybody was sleeping, she came to my bed and she started molesting me. Incest is detestable to any family, because it brings reproach and shame on the family. Incest is evil to its very root. I was always afraid to speak out against the abuse that was being done to me by my family members. Fear paralyzed my very life and put me in great bondage to many things. I was scared to speak up for myself, because I was programmed at a very early age to fear men. That was my foundation—to fear men so they could keep on having their evil desires toward me and to keep me quiet. The enemy always wants the evil things done to you kept in the dark to keep you in bondage, but when the evil is exposed and comes to light, it loses its power over you and your enemies no longer control you. I now have the victory over these things. My family never talked about family struggles or problems from within. They never revealed family secrets like my uncle raping his brother's wife. That was devastating for me to hear as an adult, because I had no clue until my uncle's wife told me. This is why the family is so dysfunctional. To this day, some family members are in denial about certain things that have happened in the family. Healing comes forth after secrets are revealed from past hurts and violations. I want to reveal some things that I struggled with called the after math.

I had some sexual identity problems and identity issues after I was raped and molested as a young child. I became promiscuous at an early age and completely out of control in every area of my life because of what happened to me. The very first time I [9]was raped in that abandoned building, evil spirits entered into me—a spirit of fear, a spirit of control and a spirit of perversion. I could not think for myself. When all of these things happened to me I did not know what I was really dealing with until later in my adult life when I became a born again Christian.

As a teenager, I became sexually active without a husband, which was not good at all. A healthy sexual relationship is between a married woman and a married man and both are protected under God's law as one in unity. I started getting very confused about being with women or being with men. This was that spirit of perversion that entered my body when my female cousin was violating me. This is one of the many reasons Satan can gain a stronghold in our lives—also through generational curses. A generational curse is when your ancestors who existed before you began practicing incest, homosexuality, alcohol, drugs, murder, sexual misconduct, witchcraft, rape, idol worshiping, prejudice and slavery. Sometimes these behaviors can be passed down from generation to generation. Each generation get passed down to is worse than the last. The curse keeps passing down to each generation for the destruction of the family unit. This is the plan that Satan has—for all the families on earth to self-destruct. The very things that happened in my life before my deliverance.

---

[8]   …This battle is not for the strong. Ecclesiastes 9:11Paraphrased

[9]   I am delivered in Jesus name. Mark 16:9

Listen people of America and all over the world, God did not create you to be with the same sex. He loves you so much, He sent His only begotten Son to die for the world. Instead of judging and persecuting the gays and lesbians. Christians should pray for them and love them. You are to draw them with love and kindness. Has He not drawn you with love and kindness? Love the people, but hate the sin. It keeps people isolated and they cannot receive their deliverance. Before we became Christians, we were doing things [10] under the sun and now we think we are so holy we cannot help anybody else get to heaven. How sad is that? You never know what causes a person to lead the lifestyle they have chosen. Some people's pain is unspeakable or unapproachable because of shame and guilt.

My mind and life was filled with nothing but confusion. I did not have the family support system nor did I have a female role model to teach me how to keep my own body clean or teach me the importance of an education. I learned all these things the hard way!

Today there is hope for every child, teenager and adult out there who has suffered any kind of abuse. I want you to know that I understand your hurt and pain and what happened to you is not your fault. Find someone you can trust to talk to and start your healing process. I have to tell you that your healing will not come overnight. It will take time, so be patient with yourself and get the help you need. I am coming forth with the truth about my childhood. I do not want a dark cloud hanging over my children's heads because of evil family secrets. It is my duty to protect them by revealing the truth. I suffered in silence, but not anymore. I was an easy target for anybody and everybody, but I have the victory!

People can smell fear and intimidation on a person just like an animal can when it is seeking out its prey. They use that to their advantage. The strong preying on the weak is inhuman and as evil as a heathen witch. We have a responsibility to stand up for those who cannot stand up for themselves. Let us take a stand on this matter.

I did not care about school or an education because I could not focus. I can remember when I was in elementary school; I was very withdrawn from teachers and [11] students. I did not trust anybody because everybody I loved and trusted had hurt me. It was very hard for me to learn in the classroom. I had a special teacher everyday. I had a wonderful teacher named Ms. Thomas. She taught me how to read, write and tell time. Ms. Thomas was so gentle and loving. I will never forget her acts of kindness.

I want everyone who is reading this book to remember that reading is a gift. People perish because of a lack of knowledge. This is for people of all ages. Don't let the computer do the thinking for you. A mind is a terrible thing to waste. Computers are great in their respective places, but we must utilize our minds.

I began living from place to place after I was put out of my grandmother's house. I lived with this old man and his younger girl friend. He drank like a fish and his girlfriend drank a lot, too. Rob started sexually harassing me all the time when nobody was watching. I hated it with a passion, but at the time, I did not have anywhere else to go. I would not be alone in a room with Rob for my own protection. This old man often verbally and physically abused his girlfriend.

He had a nephew named Jeremy. This man was so wild I was scared of him. Jeremy met this Christian woman named Dawn and they became a couple and got married. Jeremy was a hell raiser and an alcoholic. He was very controlling of his wife to the point that he started abusing

---

[10]   Always keep a servants heart, and love God's people.

[11]   …Put not your trust in man, but put your trust in God. Jere 17:5-8 paraphrased

her physically and emotionally and taking her money. I felt so bad for Dawn, yet I could not help her. One day while Jeremy was out doing God knows what he got into a brawl with a man who stabbed Jeremy to death. This was very sad for me because he was so young, but he lived in the fast lane. It is true that if you live by the sword, you die by the sword.

Finally , I left Rob's house. There was too much confusion going on and I found no peace. I met this young man named Dan. We started talking and became a couple. I [12] began spending a lot of time at his house. I was around thirteen years old at the time. I cared for Dan, but I was not in love with him. I did not know exactly what love was at the time. I was looking for love in all the wrong places. I stayed with Dan for a little while then we split up.

I meet this girl named Doreen. Her mother was an evangelist. Doreen and I became best friends and we were like sisters. Doreen's mother took me into her home and took care of me like one of her own children. Ms. Claudia had thirteen children of her own. Most of them were grown. Ms. Claudia had three minor children still living at home with her. Doreen was three years older than I was and we went everywhere together, including church. We started spending the night at her other brother's and sister's houses. We started running the streets together. I began dating her cousin. He was all right, but I liked the other cousin better, so I started dating him and broke up with the first one. I really liked him but it just was not in the cards. Often men took advantage of my vulnerability and I was oblivious to life.   (Undiscerning of what was happening to me).

When I was fifteen, I met this twenty-seven year old man named Wilson. He was married at the time, but they were separated. Wilson was seeing my cousin's friend. I really liked what I saw and wanted him for myself. I learned that my cousin's friend had sex with him on the first night they met. Many men really don't respect a woman after they get the goods on the first night. Wilson and I started talking. That's all it was for a while. Two months later Wilson and I were involved. We had a serious relationship going on—at least I thought we did. It is never okay to be with another woman's husband or be with another man's wife. It hurts so many people and destroys lives.

[13] I did not learn any morals or values as a child. I learned to do everything that was wrong in society. I did the exact thing my mother did—took someone else's husband and tried to make him my own. You can't take what belongs to somebody else without consequences. Do not covet what belongs to someone else. Just because there is, no law against adultery does not make it right.

Wilson and I began seeing a lot of each other. We started hanging out with Doreen and our other friend Freda. Bill had a brother named Darnell. I introduced him to Doreen and they started liking each other. Darnell and Doreen became a couple and we all started hanging out together. Then Freda met the older brother named Shelby. They started liking each other. We were three friends dating three brothers. We started cooking for each other and having a good time.

I had this friend named Kia. She was in her early twenties at that time. I was around fourteen when I started hanging out with her. Kia had a live-in boyfriend with a nice house. I liked going over there because they gave parties sometimes. Before I met Bill, I was dating her brother, Kelly. I thought he was very gentle toward me and he liked me a lot. However, he was too young for me at the time. I started seeing Kelly's brother, Todd who was married with two children.

One night Todd and I went to a motel to spend time together and his wife was looking for him. That next morning we left the hotel for him to drop me off. We saw his mother and she

---

[12]   Looking for love in all the wrong places.
[13]   …God teaches me all things. 1John 2:27 paraphrased

went back and told his wife that he was with me. Todd's wife came to the woman's house I was living with at the time to confront me about her husband. That woman slapped me so hard I saw stars. Todd stopped her from assaulting me further. There is an old saying that you reap what you sow in this life, and I got what I deserved.

[14] There was one night when I went over to Kia's house and I got drunk and could not walk on my own. Kia had another brother named Roger, and he tried to rape me because he knew I was drunk. Roger kept pulling on my clothes and touching me in an inappropriate way. I threw up all over Kia's house because I was drunk. At this point, my whole life was a mess.

After Wilson and I started dating, Kia told me that her brother, Todd was shot to death trying to rob a store. What a tragedy and loss. I got pregnant by Wilson at age fifteen and he was twenty-seven years old. We started living with his mother and I got on welfare to help support my unborn child. This is what I grew up around—the women in my family on welfare to support their children. It was a generational curse of poverty, but thank God for the welfare system. Children are a product of their ancestors until they grow up and see the error of their ways sadly some never do.

Wilson's mom talked me into letting her hold the money I was saving for my unborn child. She spent my money on alcohol and cigarettes and I never got it back. That was a slap in the face for me because I trusted her. Wilson came to me while I was pregnant and asked if he could borrow a hundred dollars. He said that he would pay it back before I had the baby. I never got that money back either. When you are a child with no parents to care for you, people take advantage of you. This is a very cold world.

Finally , I went into the hospital to have my baby. After she was born, I lost pints of blood and had to have a blood transfusion. I went from a size twelve to a six. My baby girl and I were released from the hospital and stayed at Wilson's mom house for a little while.

[15] I remember one night when my daughter was around three months old. Wilson went out to the store to get the baby some milk. He did not come back until the next day. Wilson spent the night with some woman while his daughter went hungry. Wilson had a reputation for being violent. Everybody was scared of him, including me. One day Wilson and I were walking and talking. He told me a story about a man that used to walk up and down the street where we lived. Wilson went to a friend of his and told him that this man was trying to molest his daughter, but Perry did not make a big deal out of it because he knew the man was slow. Wilson started saying, "I know you are not going to let him get away with trying to molest your daughter." Therefore, Perry pulled out a gun, shot, and killed the man. All because of the peer pressure he felt, a man was murdered. The man who was murdered was not a threat to anyone. I used to see him walking all the time and he never tried to harm me. Wilson was actually bragging and laughing about the murder. I moved out of Wilson's motherhouse and moved in with my aunt for a while.

One night I went out with Doreen, my aunt kept my daughter for me. Wilson was over at my aunt's house while I was out. He got into an argument with my cousin because she pushed me when I was pregnant and he slapped her in the face and spat on her. My cousin was wrong for what she did to me, but Wilson was even more wrong for seeking revenge. I decided to go visit my aunt in California. At the time, I was sixteen years old and my daughter was four months old.

---

[14] Be sober, be vigilant; because your adversary the devil, as a roaring lion, walketh about, seeking whom he may devour: 1 Peter 5:8

[15] God always takes care of the innocent babies!

When I got to L.A. I stayed with my aunt and her new husband. My Aunt Lisa married a much younger man. He was young enough to be her son. Ralph was in and out of jail. He was also addicted to crack cocaine. My Aunt Lisa started doing crack cocaine shortly after they got married. I did not feel comfortable in that environment with [16] my daughter. One day when Aunt Lisa was smoking crack, she asked me to try some. I said, "No thank you," but she was very persistent and she kept trying. One time she blew crack in my face to try to get me high and strung out. The only thing I could think about was my daughter. Any type of street drug is bad for you. I had sense enough to rebel against the drugs because I knew it would have destroyed my life.

This is to all the parents across America. You are a parent to your children and not their friend. That will come, as they get older. Know whom your children are hanging around with and where they are at all times. Children cannot rear themselves. I believe that children should have some freedom, but freedom comes with responsibility. Hold your children accountable when they do wrong because children need guidance. Don't be passive about it. I guarantee in the end your children will rise up and call you blessed. Also, praise your children when they do well and be there for them. I did not have a family support system. That is exactly what children need. If they don't have a family support system they will find other support—like having sex, taking drugs, stealing, entering into occult practices and joining gangs. Parents we must help support our children's dreams and show them how to get there.

As a result, my aunt and her husband-smoking crack, they were evicted. They could not pay their rent. All the money they had coming in went toward buying drugs. Any addiction can and will destroy a family—like gambling, alcohol, sex, pornography, money, food and drugs.

I had to leave and go back to my hometown with my seven-month-old daughter. When I got back to my hometown, I was under the impression that Wilson and I were still together as a couple. I started living with my best friend Doreen's brother and his wife. [17] One night I went out to an after-hours joint and saw Wilson there with another woman. I asked him who that woman was. Wilson did not like the idea of me questioning him and he put his hands around my throat and started choking me. At that point, I knew he was crazy and had no respect for women. I left him alone after he got violent with me. I started moving on with my life and started seeing another man I had previously dated. This young man always liked me know matter what. Wilson started coming around me again after he got bored with the woman that he was seeing at the time. I don't know how he knew I was seeing another man. It was none of his business who I was seeing because it was over between us. Wilson and the young man I was seeing got into an argument when I was not around. As far as I knew, they never liked each other, but my boyfriend stayed out of Wilson's way. Then on another occasion, they got into another argument and he assaulted my boyfriend. Now Wilson at the time was twenty-nine years old and my boyfriend was seventeen.

The young man who Wilson assaulted went and got his sister and brother to deal with the situation. They came over to my aunt's house where Wilson and I were staying at that time. There was a knock on the door. My cousin answered the door and let four people in the house—the young man who was assaulted, his sister and brother, and a friend of theirs. The young man with the gun came in the back where Wilson and I were sitting with our daughter, pulled out a gun and shot Wilson while he was holding our daughter in his arms. Then someone came and got my daughter out of his arms and Wilson stumbled into the front room. At that point, he was beaten kicked and punched by the

---

[16]   God gives us freedom to choose, choose the good.

[17]   Stay away from wrong, damaging relationships.

other suspects. I was in shock and disbelief at what was going on then the young man went over to him, pointed the gun at Wilson's head and pulled the trigger. He shot him in [18] the head. Then he pointed the gun at me. I was starring at the barrel of the gun. I thought 'I'm dead now,' but for some reason he did not pull that trigger. I believe that Almighty God protected me from being destroyed for a higher purpose. The police were called. By the time they arrived, Wilson was dead. The hardest thing I had to do was to call Wilson's mom and tell her that her son was dead. Wilson's mom was asking me all kinds of questions that I was not mentally prepared for. I was still in shock and disbelief as I watched his lifeless body, lying on the floor with blood all around it.

I was only seventeen years old when this happened and my daughter was turning one-year-old five days after Wilson's death. The police questioned me because I was an eyewitness to the murder. The next thing I knew, all of Wilson's family members were calling me and asking me about what happened to him. This was very overwhelming for me as a young girl who had just witnessed a murder. I told them what happened as best as I could in my state of mind. I felt empty, lost and hurt over what happened to my daughter's father. I never wanted anything bad to happen to Wilson at any time. Wilson was wrong for assaulting this young man, but they were even more wrong for killing Wilson. Violence never solves anything, because it hurts so many other people—both sides of the family, friends and children.

I was summoned to go to court and testify against the young man who killed Wilson because I was the eyewitness and saw the whole thing. This was very hard for me because I was so scared of what would happen to me after my testimony. Instead of me getting love and support for what I was going through, Wilson's mother and the majority of the family blamed me. I was very hurt and confused by the accusations that I was responsible.

[19] Wilson 's mother and family disowned my daughter. I had to go through this situation by myself with very little support. When all of this was going on I met Wilson's aunt, and she did not share the same thoughts as the rest of her family. Yes, Wilson was murdered at my aunt's house, but I had no control over the situation at all. My daughter's aunt allowed me to move in with her, and she accepted my daughter as her flesh and blood. My daughter's grandmother was constantly calling and harassing her sister because she opened up her home to my daughter and me. She disowned her sister because of the love she was showing to us.

During the arrangements of Wilson's funeral, my daughter's grandmother did not mention her own grandchild in the obituary. My thoughts and feelings on that is that it was cruel and evil to take her guilty conscience out on an innocent child. A couple months before Wilson died; his mother revealed to him in a drunken state that the man he thought all those years was his father was not his father at all. Wilson was so hurt and broken up about it he started crying right in front of me. I believe the reason why she took Wilson's death so hard is that she never had a chance to redeem herself or tell Wilson she was sorry for what she put him through. Keeping dark family secrets destroys any family.

I did take my daughter to her father's funeral because she had every right to be there—just as much as the rest of the family. Wilson served in the Marine Corp and was buried in Marine garments. The funeral was so crowded it was standing room only. I did not go to his casket to view the body because of the animosity the family felt toward my daughter and me.

---

[18]   When I cry unto thee, then shall mine enemies turn back: this I know for God is for me. Psalm 56:9

[19]   …You are no more bastards, but sons of God. Hebrews 12:7-8 Paraphrased

[20] The murder trial began. The courtroom was closed to the public because of the young man's age. Wilson's family was not allowed in the courtroom at all. I was out in the hallway waiting for the judge to call me to testify as to what I had witnessed. Wilson's mom and family were in the hallway waiting. I was frightened of them because I knew they hated me without cause.

Finally , I was called into the courtroom to testify about the murder. Out of everybody that was in my aunt's house at the time of Wilson's murder, I was the only one they called to testify against the young man. The prosecutor asked me to state my name and what I witnessed February of 1986. The prosecutor asked if the murderer was in the room, and asked if I could point him out, I did. The jury convicted the young man of Wilson's murder, and the judge gave him twenty-five years to life in prison.

I did fear for my life after I testified against that young man. I really thought the family was going to come after me because I put him in prison. In reality, I was scared of Wilson's family and the young man's family. Can you imagine my life being shattered and confused with no one to trust?

After the trial was over, my cousin, who tried to rape me told me that the young man I put in prison told him that he was going to kill me. Imagine that. I believe that my cousin wanted me dead because he could not have his way with me sexually.

I stayed in the city for about a year after Wilson's death. I started living with my best friend, Doreen's brother and his wife. That did not go very well because he tried to get extra money out of me that I did not have. Doreen's brother grabbed me physically and started searching for money that I had put away for my daughter. This man even [21] searched my bra to find the money and he stole my money. I felt so violated and betrayed. I took my daughter and I left. All this happened shortly after my daughter's father was killed. I have had people like that take advantage of me my whole life. Doreen's mother went to her son who stole my money, got it back from him, and gave it back to me. I am so thankful for Doreen's mother. I respected and loved her greatly. She was an honorable woman who loved people.

for as long as people and time have existed, the strong have preyed on the weak. I always had people prey on me as a very young child and into my adult life. I was too weak to stand up for myself when people abused me. At this stage in my life, I will never let anyone ever abuse me again.

I met this man named Jimmy and we started dating. Then we started getting serious and formed a relationship. We moved from the city to start our relationship. It was all right in the beginning stage, but when it came down to it he was scared of responsibility. I got pregnant by him and had a beautiful little girl.

I want everybody to know that playing house without really being married is a devastating thing because we are not giving our children a solid foundation to stand on. It is sin in God's eyes and there is no spiritual protection. Those that commit adultery and fornication sin against their own body.

During the time I lived in L.A., I received some court papers in the mail from Wilson's other children's mother. She was claiming that my daughter was not Wilson's daughter and therefore was trying to stop my daughter from getting survivor benefits that rightfully belonged to her. This was a huge court case. My daughter's grandmother was behind the whole thing. It was testimony after testimony with Wilson's mother and other [22] family members. I was not in the same city with them when this was going on. I was still in L.A. I consulted legal council in L.A. and the

---

[20] Thou shalt not kill. Ex 20:13
[21] My treasure is in the Lord!
[22] God is a lawyer when you need one, and there is no charge.

case continued for months. Debbie perjured herself on the stand because she kept changing her story. My daughter did have two relatives from Wilson's family to testify on her behalf. I have to say that the true and living God was on my side the whole time because documentation of proof surfaced in the courtroom. There was a legal document from Veteran's Affairs submitted to the court as evidence that my daughter was in fact his daughter. The case against my daughter was dismissed. God will fight your battles for you. How could a mother who claims to love her son so much hate her own grandchild? All the things this woman put me through were from a wicked and evil heart.

shortly after all that happened, my daughter's grandmother died. I have always been hated by people without cause, now I know why—hated by man, but loved by God. After I heard about her passing, I felt no remorse at all and the reason was that she sowed lies and it spread like cancer. I did forgive her for the damage she caused to my daughter. To this day, my daughter's aunts and uncles reject her as if she is nothing. My daughter looks exactly like her aunt and oldest brother. I say to everybody in my daughter's family who rejected her that it is your loss, not hers. Resentment and hatred will make anybody's life hell if they do not repent.

Both of my daughters are beautiful young women who are going places in life. I forgive my daughter's family and everybody else for hurting me, stealing from me and any other evil acts that was committed against me. I see now that all the pain and suffering I went through was to help multitudes of people.

[23] Any family members that are out there at this very moment who hold hate and resentment in their heart toward another family member or anybody else go to God in humbleness, ask Him to forgive you for holding bitterness and unforgiveness in your heart, then go to that person, and ask for forgiveness. Do not let pride stop you from doing the right thing. Pride goes before destruction and a haughty spirit before a fall. Forgive everybody who has trespassed against you. It will not only profit you, but your entire family. When we have evil intentions to harm others in our heart and act it out, it brings generational curses on the family. In the bible God said, "I have set before you blessing and cursing—you chose." (Deuteronomy 30: 19

I love my children very much even though I did not always know how to show it to my oldest daughter because no one ever showed me how to love. God showed me His perfect love working in my life over the years. That is how I became a good mom. I protected my children from men or anyone else who preyed on the innocent and vulnerable. That is why sexual predators prey on the weak. It is our job as parents to protect, love and teach our children the way they should go. It is not the responsibility of the public schools and society to teach our children because teaching always starts in the home. Children don't often follow what we say but what we do. What we should do is lead our children by example. I don't know if you are aware of this but everybody in this world sets some kind of example for people of all ages—friends, preachers, teachers, pastors, managers, mothers, fathers, aunts, uncles, cousins, mentors, advocates, social workers, greeters, presidents, false teachers, false prophets and false Christ's. What kind of example or impression are you leading for those around you? I can remember when I was a child and all these horrible evil things happened to me because of no love, no teaching and no [24]guidance. There were people around me but they were setting all the wrong examples and giving me all the wrong impressions. I saw the examples of alcoholics, drug

---

[23]   …Forgive those who have trespassed against you. Matthew 6:14-15 Paraphrased.

[24]   Jesus set the example when He died for our sins.

addicts, prostitutes, child molesters, rapists, party animals, confusion, neglectful parenting, sexual immorality, violence, incest, poverty, lack of character and adultery. I now teach what is right and what is wrong. I now help people to know who they are and how valuable they are in God's eyes and I now know how to show the love of Christ.

In the church, I have experienced control, condemnation, hurt and spiritual assassination. "God has not called you to be an evangelist," they said. I will share that God has not called any leader to abuse his or her congregation or have control over them. They are to lead by example, preach and teach the Word, not their own doctrine. This also destroys lives, that is why attendance is low in some churches, because the people are being condemned and abused, and this needs to stop! God is not pleased. There is no condemnation in Christ Jesus; Romans 8:1

I had to find a way to get out of prison and start living my life. In my mind, I was in prison and held captive by a spirit of fear. Fear brings torment. Even though I left my hometown to start life over again, I still had some serious issues and problems that I did not discover until years later.

I know that some people would say that whatever happened to me as a child, I should be over it. You can still be scared, deeply hurt and deeply wounded by things and you may not even know it. You think you are healed until something comes along in your life to trigger that pain all over again. All those old feelings and memories start coming back again and you feel helpless.

[25] I was very happy when I started dealing with my own issue and what was wrong with me and identify that with the true and living God. Healing is a process and it does not happen over night. For some it takes longer than others. I am living proof you do not have to be like your mother or your father or any other family member that has set the wrong examples. I did cut evil ties that had me bound for so long.

Anybody out there who is going through similar situations stop blaming yourself and start the healing process for you and your children. I always felt intimidated with anyone who had power and control because people in a position of trust abused me. I still fight with that to this day. People ran over me as a child and young adult. I did not speak out against anything. I learned how to speak up when I saw the strong preying on the weak.

When I was twenty-two years old, my second daughter was born in California. Then I moved to Colorado when she was four months old. I met this man named Brian. We started talking because I thought he was a nice man to be around. It started good but turned bad when he tried to control me. I learned that this man had a serious problem with a woman being independent and thinking for herself. Two months into the relationship Brian said, "Marry me." I looked at him as if he was crazy, because it was too soon to marry this man. In addition, the more I was around him; the less I liked his character.

One night I was at Brian's house. He started assaulting me by punching and slapping me, throwing me up against the wall and would not let me leave. I was tormented all that night. Then he let me go. I did not go to the police because I was too scared to press charges. Finally, I told Brian that I never wanted to see him again. It was [26] over. Brian did not take rejection very well. He went to the leasing office where I was renting and told my manager that I was selling drugs out of my apartment to try to get me evicted. I had children, but do you think he cared about that? This man was out to ruin my life anyway he could. My manager did not believe his story about me selling drugs. That was a lie Brian told to get me and the children put out.

---

25 I was the woman at the well. John 4: 6-18 paraphrased
26 People will reject you, but God says …He will never leave you nor forsake you. Hebrews 13:5

My manager suggested that I get a restraining order on Brian because she saw him becoming a potential problem for me. I did get a temporary restraining order and a date was set for a permanent restraining order. When Brain was served the order of protection, he went crazy and started stalking me and coming over to my house. The police were called. They did not catch him. He was watching the police and when they left, he came right back and broke out all my windows in a very violent way. Thank God, I was living on the second floor because he tried to break in my house several times but failed.

The police finally did catch him and Brian was charged with breaking an order of protection, vandalism and trespassing. The court ordered him to pay me restitution for the damages he caused. In the mean time, I had to pay for my windows to be replaced. When Brian was stalking me, there was no law against it. He was following me everywhere. I was very frightened.

I remember when I was staying with my aunt and Brian came over to visit me. It turned violent with him giving me a black eye. My daughters were in the room sleeping. I ran out of the house for help. Brian left and locked my daughters in the apartment. I was scared that he did something to them. Thank God, my girls were safe. Eventually stalking became against the law and Brian started being arrested for stalking and breaking the restraining order. One night Brian was at my house and he [27]started calling me names and threatening me. Then he hit me and I grabbed a butcher knife and cut him with it for my own protection. Brian called the police and told me that I was going to jail for cutting him. When the officer got there, he saw Brian bleeding and asked me what happened. I told him I cut him out of self-defense. The officer said he could take me to jail right then for assault. I told the officer that this man did not live there and I wanted him out of my house. The officer escorted Brian off the property and I was not charged.

I did get back with Brian out of fear only, not love, but that did not stop the abuse. I can remember one night when he beat me, called me all kinds of names and threw me up against the wall. Then he raped me. When a woman is being battered on a regular basis, she cannot think for herself at all.

In the state of mind that I was in, I took care of my children as best I could. At one point, I almost lost my girls to the state because of this low-life man. I was determined that I was not going to lose my children because I loved them with everything that I had in me. Brian was so manipulating. When he got charged for assaulting me and breaking the restraining order, he would talk me into dropping the charges and writing a statement that it was a mistake. All the court records on what Brian did to me are in the court files to this day.

Now in domestic violence cases when a man batters a woman and she does not press charges, the state automatically picks up the charges. That is what happened in Brian's case. One night I had my door open enjoying my peace and here comes Brian. He said, "I just want to talk to you."

[28] I said, "I have nothing to say to you. Leave my house." Brian forced his way in and started hitting me. My oldest daughter came in and said, "Leave my mommy alone!"

He said he would not hurt me and I know that was a lie! I managed to get outside and Brian tried to pull me and kick me down a flight of concrete stairs. I was holding on for dear life to the

---

[27]   God is my protection!

[28]   …If you live by the sword, you will die by the sword. Matthew 26:52

rail. The police came, caught him in the act, and took him to jail. I was pregnant at the time that Brian tried to pull me down those stairs. I believe he was trying to kill me.

Brian found out that I was pregnant and tried to use that to remain in my life to control me and abuse me. I told him I wanted nothing to do with him ever again. I was confused about getting an abortion. I did not believe in abortion, but I was thinking about keeping this maniac out of my life for good. I decided to bring the baby to full term and give the baby up for adoption. I met the woman, who wanted to adopt my baby, but she said something to me and I changed my mind instantly. The thought of me being abused made me change my mind.

While I was pregnant, Brian got a restraining order on me. It was not for his protection but to bring false accusations against me so I would go to jail. I went to court and signed the restraining order to keep him away from me. One afternoon when I was at home with my girls, I was eight months pregnant and there was a knock on the door. It was two police officers, one male and one female. The female officer asked me if I was R.I. I told her yes and she said she was sorry but they had come to arrest me for breaking a restraining order. They asked if I was on or around Mallard Drive that day. I said that I had been home with my children all day. I told the officer that I did not have a car to get there even if I wanted to. I also told the officer that I had been repeatedly harassed and [29] assaulted by this man and wanted nothing to do with him. The two officers talked among themselves and the female officer came back and said they believed me and were not going to arrest me. I was very relieved because I was concerned about my girls being taken away on a false charge.

One day I woke up and decided I was not going to be a victim anymore and I went to the pawnshop and bought a small handgun. I carried this gun with me everywhere I went for protection. One day I decided to lure Brian over to my house by pretending to want him back so that I could kill him and he could never hurt me again. Brian agreed to come over. I had the gun under my pillow to kill him.

When he came over, we went into my bedroom talking and shooting the breeze. He found the gun under the pillow, his eyes got big and he asked what I was doing with a gun. I had to think fast and said that it belonged to my friend who lived in the same apartments I did. I told Brian to give me the gun so I could take it to my friend. He did and I took it out of the house. This could have been a very tragic day for my children and I Brian could have killed all of us with my own gun. Instead, he was very scared and surprised that I had that gun. From that day forward, Brian never bothered me again, but he still had charges he was facing for what he did to me.

Violence is never the answer to solve problems. I know today that it was the Lord protecting me and my children in that gun situation. God says that vengeance is His. I will repay saith the Lord.

When Brian went to court for those charges he was facing, they gave him six months in jail. After he did his time, the State of Colorado told him to leave and never to [30] return or he would be doing life in prison. Brian left and never returned to the state of Colorado. He moved to Washington and died there.

I had a beautiful baby boy and he is fourteen years old. He is very smart and he loves to play basketball. I teach my son not to ever hit women because of what I've been through. I also shared with him what his biological father did so he will not make the same mistakes. It is never

---

[29] Whoso diggeth a pit shall fall therein… Proverbs 26: 27

[30] God separated us forever!

all right for a woman or a man to get violent for any reason. Walk away because somebody could be killed or seriously hurt.

Young women that are in middle school and high school, it is not all right for you to hit, kick, punch or harass the young men in your school and think you can hide behind the teachers when the heat is on. If boys are suspended for this issue, so should girls because some of the time it is the girl that is in violation of physical assault. It should be dealt with accordingly. According to the statistics, violence is on the rise among females so when a female cries wolf make sure you have solid proof. If not, watch the female and the accuser to determine who is guilty.

Out of all my relatives who knew that I had a bad childhood, only one person in my family came and apologized to me for the pain and suffering I endured. That was my uncle who once beat me. I looked at him as if he was crazy. My uncle and his wife came to live with me while I was in a domestically violent relationship until they got their own place to live.

One day when I was at his house (this was years later) the conversation came up about my childhood. He said, "I'm sorry for everything you went through as a child. I did not know what it was like for you."[31]

His apology really touched me because I was not expecting it. Nobody ever apologized to me before for hurting me. I believe God showed my uncle the truth about what happened to me as a child because he was only told bad things about me—that I was a bad girl. My uncle had tears running down his face when he apologized. It was a heart-felt apology.

Now, my uncle has passed on to be with the Lord. He was saved two weeks before he passed. I was a witness and heard his confession to the Lord. I was the minister at his funeral and it was such a blessing and privilege to be there for him going home. Some people misunderstand who I am and they prejudge me before they really know my character. To know me is to love me, and I do not take that for granted because I know what it is like to be rejected, abused, hurt wounded and left for dead. Now people are drawn to me. Not because I am good, but because the Greater One is in me and all good things come from above. Therefore, when people are drawn to me it is because God has something for them through me that He wants them to have.

I have been through many things and that is why I have a great call on my life as an evangelist. I am called to the hurt, lost, those who have been rejected and those who have been wounded by the church to do the will of my heavenly Father. The world showed me no love, but God showed me His agape love and that I have a great future in Him.

Only recently, God has placed me with some of His finest people to continue to help build what He started. I walked alone for many years and was rejected by many in the church as I sought the Lord and what He would have me to do in the Kingdom. I was in prayer everyday like clockwork and the Holy Spirit revealed to me that I am His [32] evangelist and I accepted the call. I was already doing evangelism work at the church I was going to at that time, in 1999. Now, I am married to a wonderful man and he supports the evangelistic call on my life. Between us, we have six children.

I believe that God is going to bless us with many spiritual children to teach and to love. I thank God that I am more than a conquer over the evil situations I went through. I thank God for my true spiritual family because I never had a real family to call my own. I give God all the glory, praise and honor for allowing me to write this book!

---

31 God revealed the truth to my uncle before he passed.

32 …Do the work of an evangelist… 2Timothy 4: 5

This book is dedicated to all the people around the world who are suffering from situations similar to the ones from which God has delivered and healed me. This book will touch and change multitudes of people's lives.

[33] EACH PRECIOUS STONE REPRESENTS THE TWELVE TRIBES OF ISRAEL! EXODUS 28: 16-21
Each precious stone was used for Aaron's breastplate Ex   28:17-20
Define each precious stone.
(SARDIUS)

(TOPAZ)

(CARBUNCLE)

(EMERALD)

(SAPPHIRE)

(DIAMOND)

(LIGURE)

(AGATE)

(AMETHYST)

(BERYL)

(ONYX)

(JASPER)
(Contact Information)
Email: evangelistclark@live.com
Witnessing With Power
P.O. Box 25823
Colorado Springs, Colorado 80936-5823

---

[33]   All these stones were real and very costly.

ARE YOU EMOTIONALLY DAMAGED?

Take the survey to find out.

1. Have any of your family members at anytime belittled you constantly?

2. Have you been rejected by your parents as a child?

3. Were you abused by your parents as a child?

4. Where you ever bullied at school?

5. Have you ever been controlled by anyone and you lost your idenity?

6. Have you been emotionally abused by anyone?

7. Have you ever been sexually abused?

8. Have you ever been raped by a stranger?

9. Have you ever been raped by a family member?

10. Have you ever been raped by a family friend?

11. Have you ever suffered from a sexual identity crisis such as homosexuality?

12. Have you ever lost your identity as a person not knowing who you are?

13. Were you ever abused by your friends?

14. Have you ever been in a domestic violent relationship?

15. Have you ever been date raped before?

16. Were you adopted and suffered abuse?

17. Have you ever been in foster care before?

18. Are you contemplating suicide?

19. Have you ever attempted suicide?

20. Did you grow up with no family?

21. Do you fear what people say about you?

22. Do you have healthy relationships?

23. Have you ever been abused by a person in a position of

24. Have you ever been abused by the pastor of a church?

25. Have you ever been pregnant by a pastor while he was married?

26. Have you ever been abused by church leaders?

27. Have you ever been excommunicated from a church?

28. Have you ever been frequently mistreated on the job?

29. Have you ever been sexually harassed on the job?

30. Have you ever been threatened on the job?

31. Have you ever been victimized in the court system?

32. Have you ever been victimized by the Department of Human Services?

33. Have you ever had your children taken away from you?

34. Have you ever had an abortion?

If you have answered "yes" to any of these questions you are dealing with some level of emotional damage. God loves you so much that He gave His only
Begotten Son for you and the whole world.

There is help for your healing today. Talk to God about the pain you are feeling on the inside of you that nobody sees. Also, talk to a trusted friend that will not spread your business to everybody else. We all need a support system. Remember to be patient with yourself because healing does not come over night. Do not condemn yourself or blame yourself for what has happened to you because it is not your fault. Forgive all those who have hurt you so you can receive you're full complete healing in Jesus name.

PRAYER FOR HEALING AND RESTORATION

"Our Father, who art in heaven, hallowed be thy name. Thy kingdom come, Thy will be done on earth as it is in heaven. Give us this day our daily bread. Forgive us our debts, as we forgive our debtors. And lead us not into temptation, but deliver us from evil. For thine is the kingdom, and the power, and the glory."

(Luke 11:2-4)

Father I thank you that you care for your sons and daughters equally and you have placed your sons and daughters on the earth to care for us equally. Father God, I thank you that you sent your Son to die for the whole human race and I thank you God that women have a special place in your heart and your
Kingdom. We are all made in your image and neither male nor female is superior over the other. We are to love one another, build and edify each other for this is pleasing in the Lord's sight. I pray, heavenly Father, that all the women, men, boys and girls will be healed in Jesus name and I release the blood of Jesus for salvation, healing of the spirit, healing of the mind, emotional healing, family healing and demonic healing. I pray that man's doctrine will be broken off the women so they can serve you freely in Jesus' name, Amen.

THE BENEDICTION

God kept me when all odds were stacked against me! When came in like a flood to over take me, God lifted me up a standard against him! God has placed his love inside of me, His teachings, His character, His ministry and His identity within me!

I love to do in depth study, I love to read and I love to do research. I have read over two hundred Christian books and read a lot on history, and the law! If I don't understand something I do research to find the answer. I love all of God's people male and female, but women for centuries have fallen short in society.

Women have been devalued of their self worth on the job, in their home and in church! How can this be if *"we are made in Gods image?"* *"We were all created equal in the sight of God,"* *(Genesis 1:26-27)* and we are all valued equally! There are some churches that hold women back from their full potential in Christ; this is not the will of the Father. Galatians 5: 7 says, *"ye did run well; who did hinder you that ye should not obey the truth?"*

We should always obey God rather than man, so ladies see yourselves as God sees you, valued highly in his sight. You do have a call and a purpose on this earth through God and not man!

THE MEANING OF VALUE

Excellence, greatness, respect, significance, esteem, worth, importance, usefulness, superiority. highly regarded

THE MEANING OF DEVALUE

To cause the value or importance of a person to be devalued!
Make or become less valuable.
Infect, pollute, defile, taint, corrupt, pervert, cheapen, and degrade,

CLOSING CHAPTER:

Deeply Cleansed, Deeply Valued And Deeply Loved!

THREE STEPS TO TRANSFORMATION!

STEP ONE

Deeply Cleansed! Mean to purify wash and to make whole.

I was very good at cleansing myself on thee outside but inside of me was emptiness, void of self worth and loneliness.

I remember when I use to lie to people about my education and who I was to make myself seem important so people would not judge me for who I really was. Image is everything to the world but God will accept you just as you are.

I kept the outside of me looking good but I would not go near the inside of me because it was bruised, broken and wounded.

I let God into my life for transformation!

In my earlier walk with God, I would not allow Him to come near my hurts or my faults because I was still protecting them very closely.

God was being very patient with me until I was fed up with my own shortcomings and faced myself.

Matthew 23: 25-28 was showing me exactly who I was full of greed, a hypocrite and self-indulgence.

I had to look at myself as being a hot mess in the mirror staring back at me reality hit me hard.

I started crying out to God for cleansing, healing and restoration when I noticed I was broken.

Jeremiah 33: 8 says and I will cleanse them from all their iniquity, God has cleansed me of all my wrong thinking and bad behavior this did not happen over night, God showed me things about myself little by little step by step and each time He healed me I gained ground to stand firm on His word and victory.

I learned that exposing those things that was done in the dark was very powerful and damaging to the enemy of our soul. Life hit my spirit like never before and I experienced God's unchanging hand.

Proverbs 20: 30 says the blueness of a wound cleanseth away evil: so do stripes the inward parts of the belly. This scripture for me is very significant for me because God searches out the deep part of a person, which is the heart.

While the world look upon the outward appearance God looks into your heart. God looked into my heart and found treasures of good things that only He alone could bring out of me for the good of all people. God says that I am worthy of all good things. I am deeply cleansed by the blood of Jesus and by the word of my testimony.

You can trust God to cleanse your heart He will do it with such gentleness, love and care.

Do not be concerned about what people think about you only think on the good things God is doing in your life. Philippians 4:8 whatsoever things are true whatsoever things are honest, whatsoever things are just, whatsoever things are pure, whatsoever things are lovely, whatsoever things are of good report think on these things. Fill your heart and mind with good thoughts and surround yourself with positive supportive people.

STEP TWO

Deeply valued

I believe that I am highly valued in the sight of God.

Matthew 10: 31 says fear ye not therefore ye are of more value than many sparrows.

This scripture is saying to me that we are all highly valued in the sight of God and we all have a purpose on this earth that is priceless.

I can remember when I meet my husband we dated for four years before we got married.

My husband and I both already had three children each before we meet. We started taking care of each others children and we had an extended family.

My older daughter was not happy that I got married and I started seeing resentment and resistance from her. I dealt with her as positive as I could by loving her and supporting what she wanted to do.

Finally, she forced herself out of the home before her time was come, that left four children in the home after my daughter left. I really started having major problems with my stepdaughter not listening, not obeying authority, you not my mama and was violent toward me. I decided to stay gone a lot in the beginning years of my marriage because it was too much to handle. I was still praying and some time I did not have the strength to pray and my marriage was in trouble. I was on the verge of leaving my husband, but I prayed to God first and I asked him what shall I do?

The Lord said to me love your husband and minister to him at that moment I surrendered to the word of the Lord and I asked Him to change me.

In the process of you asking God to change you God is also changing your spouse at the same time.

I started praying all the more for my husband to be blessed by God and I started seeing the value of prayer by changes I started seeing in my husband.

God is so wonderful! He showed me how valuable I am as a mother even when my children don't appreciate me as a caregiver. I am valuable as a wife because I hold my husband up with high esteem, deep respect and love for my husband.

God showed me I can love my husband and children even when they did not treat me right.

God has placed high value in me to explore in the world, in the church and in the home to have a great impact on other people's lives.

All the hurt and pain that I endured carry significant meaning of the person I have become today.

If you are going through deep, pain and hurt right now I want you to know that what you are going through is no accident but your pain is to help somebody else that you cross paths with to assist them with their healing and deliverance.

Your pain is not in vain and God will give you double for your trouble watch, believe and see.

Remember you are highly valued in God.

Since time has passed with all the family issues I know that I am loved by my children and my Husband and it keeps getting better with time.

God how awesome you are to me for showing me a more excellent way of life.

STEP THREE

Deeply Loved

John 3:16 for God so loved the world that He gave His only begotten son that whosoever believeth in Him should not perish but have ever-lasting life.

By this scripture alone I know that I am deeply loved by my heavenly Father because He sent His only son to die for my sins.

Jeremiah 29: 11 says for I know the thoughts that I think toward you, saith the Lord, thoughts of peace, and not evil to give you an expected end.

I feel like God wrote this scripture just for me Because I feel warm and highly favored from Him.

Remember when people have evil thoughts toward you that is not God, but the devil trying to impose his evil thoughts toward you reject it immediately.

Say I am highly loved by God and He has good thoughts toward me to give me an expected end!

But the fruit of the Spirit is love, joy, peace, longsuffering, gentleness, goodness, faith, meekness, temperance Galatians 5:22-23.

Many bible translations have taken the word out longsuffering no one wants to suffer with pain or misfortunes, but longsuffering produce the fruit of love, longsuffering produce godly character, longsuffering produce good ministry and long suffering cause a person to bear much fruit for the Kingdom of God.

All the longsuffering I endured over the years was Necessary for my making.

Longsuffering taught me to love, have compassion, understanding and forgiveness.

Thank you Father God for allowing my flesh to be crucified on the cross so that others may live and not die.

Why did I choose the stones on my book cover?

Exodus 28: 2-3 and thou shalt make holy garments for Aaron thy brother for glory and for beauty.

And thou shalt speak unto all that are wise hearted, whom I have filled with the spirit of wisdom, that they may make Aaron's garments to consecrate him that he may minister unto me in the priest's office. I believe that the glory of God shines upon every fiber of my being. God's beauty and glory shines within me. Romans 10:15 says and how shall they preach, except they be sent?

As it is written, how beautiful are the feet of them that preach the gospel of peace, and bring good tidings. This is exactly what God has called me to do is to preach the gospel in peace.

God traded my old worldly garments for His Glorious garment that I may minister unto Him.

Wow what a mighty powerful God we serve!

When people say that you are not worthy; Remember God has already made you worthy through Jesus shed blood on Calvary.

When I look back into my life as a child, I see God being with me and carrying me through all my challenges and bringing me out as pure gold.

God has set my feet on solid ground.

I am destined for greatness!

This is for all of my readers who read this book.

When leaders of churches don't recognize you have a call on your life or they won't allow you to use your gifts and talents in the church, don't be discouraged and don't give up what God has given you. what God has called you to do will come to pass if you faint not.

This happen to me several times from different Churches but I did not give up what God gave me.

God sent the right people into my life to activate

What was already in me purpose, destiny and wealth!

My life has been radically changed forever!

I pray that you will reach your destiny, purpose and wealth in Jesus name Amen.

All scripture came from KJV

Rachell Clark

I thank the most high God for allowing this book to come forward. I thank my husband for his support. I thank my children for their support. I thank Pastor Charles & Renee Johnson for their love and support. I thank my good friend Ray Ellis and his lovely wife. I thank Sharon Patrick for her spiritual support. I thank Carol Austin for helping with the book. I thank everyone in my life who believed in me.

Write a ten page letter on your life/struggles and ask God to help you.

Write a ten page letter on your life/struggles and ask God to help you.

Write a ten page letter on your life/struggles and ask God to help you.

Write a ten page letter on your life/struggles and ask God to help you.

Write a ten page letter on your life/struggles and ask God to help you.

Write a ten page letter on your life/struggles and ask God to help you.

Write a ten page letter on your life/struggles and ask God to help you.

Write a ten page letter on your life/struggles and ask God to help you.

Write a ten page letter on your life/struggles and ask God to help you.

Write a ten page letter on your life/struggles and ask God to help you.

Write a ten page letter on your life/struggles and ask God to help you.

NOTES

NOTES

NOTES

NOTES

NOTES

NOTES

NOTES

NOTES

Printed in the United States
By Bookmasters